I0484959

Charlotte's School Art Exhibit

Illustrated and written by
Audrey Clausen

I wrote this book to inspire not just children but also adults to use their natural talents. We all have talents that are given to us through experimenting and the willingness to explore things in life – you will find yours.

If you have already found your talent with practice, you can become the best you can be.

I encourage anyone that is reading this to find your talent and share it with others. It will not only be a blessing to you but a blessing for everyone to enjoy.

No part of this book may be reproduced or transmitted in any form or by any means, electronic or mechanical. Including photocopying, recording or by any information storage and retrieval system, without written permission from the publisher or author. For more information address 7167 74th Street Court South, Cottage Grove, MN 5501

Thank you to my loving husband Dale who has inspired me to be the best that I can be. Also, to my sweet daughters Tiffany, Brittany and Stephanie. What a blessing they are in my life! I want to always encourage them to continue on their journey of life by finding their talents and sharing them with others.

Also, to my good friend Yvonne Herman, who is always there for me, editing this book over and over. Thank you so much.

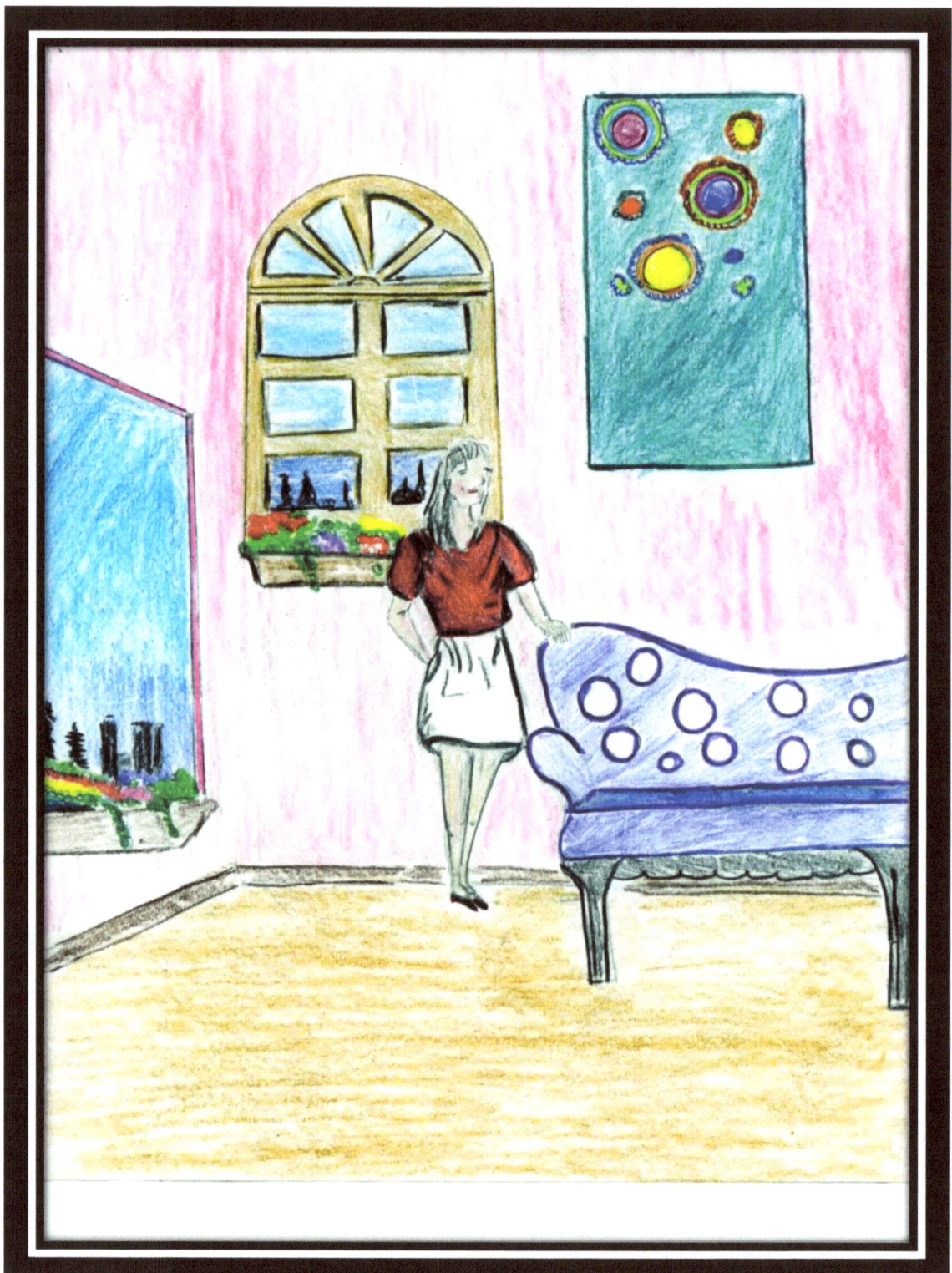

Charlotte is good at decorating. It seems that she is good at being very creative. She has a knack for making things look good. When she leaves her friends' bedrooms, she is visiting, they are pretty much revamped into fabulous boutiques, which is what her friends called their bedrooms afterwards. Her friends would say she has the "magic touch" at making anything look good. Her friends would be in awe of her decorating skills.

Charlotte visits her Grandma Bella every day after school; she has a cool art studio in her home. Most evenings her parents work. So, Charlotte would go to her Grandma's house and she would get her homework done there and then watch her Grandma paint on canvas sometimes. Her Grandma would say, "Let's paint, I will paint with you, we can paint together, Charlotte".

Grandma's paintings are beautiful. She is very good at painting. She has been an artist for many years.

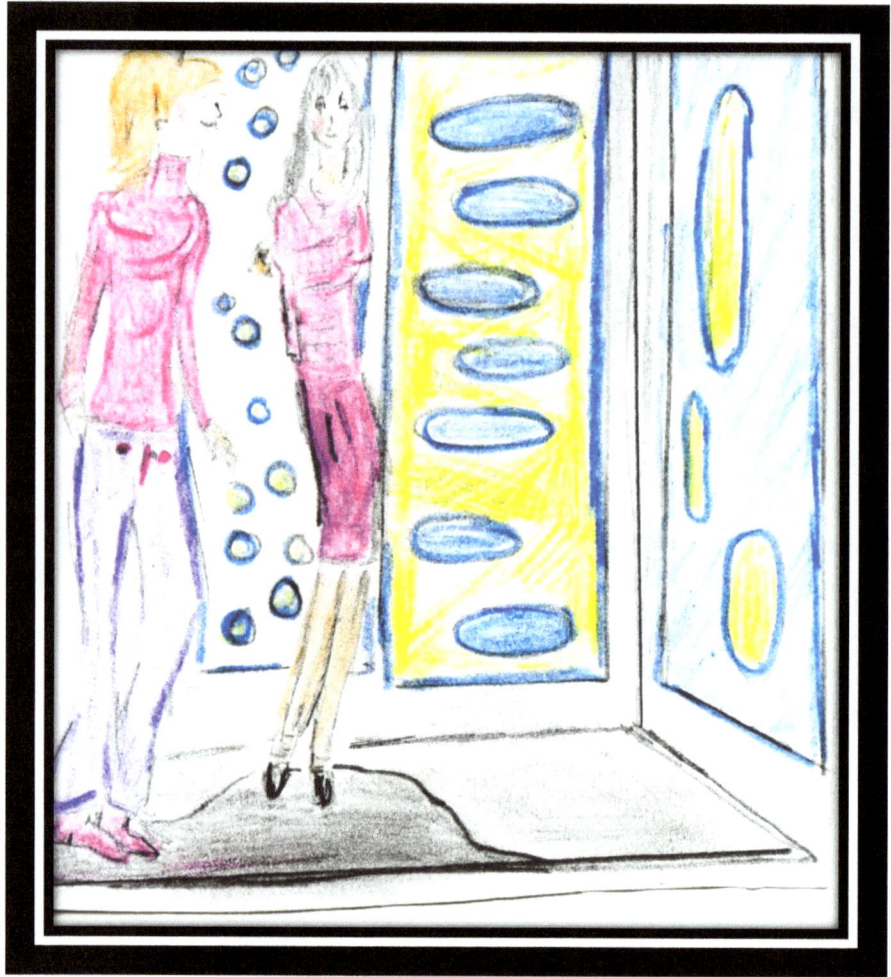

Charlotte wants to be an artist herself one day, but lacks the confidence in her paintings. Charlotte likes it when her friends say "She is good at decorating".

But once, just once, she would daydream of them saying she is a "good artist". Charlotte goes as far as dreaming of becoming a famous artist one day as she so admires the famous known artists.

These are famous artists Charlotte admired.

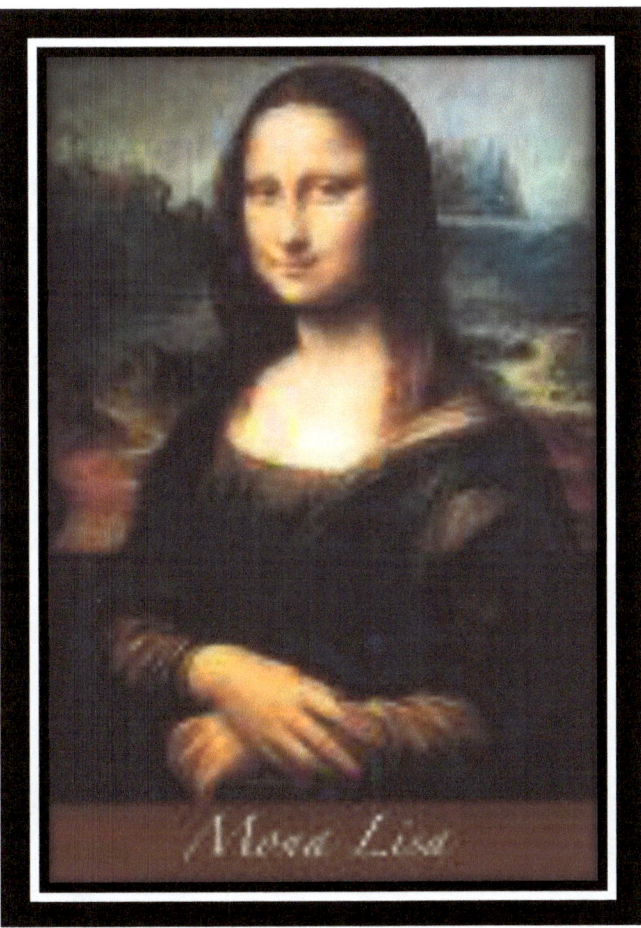

Painting of the "Mona Lisa" by Artist Leonardo da Vinci

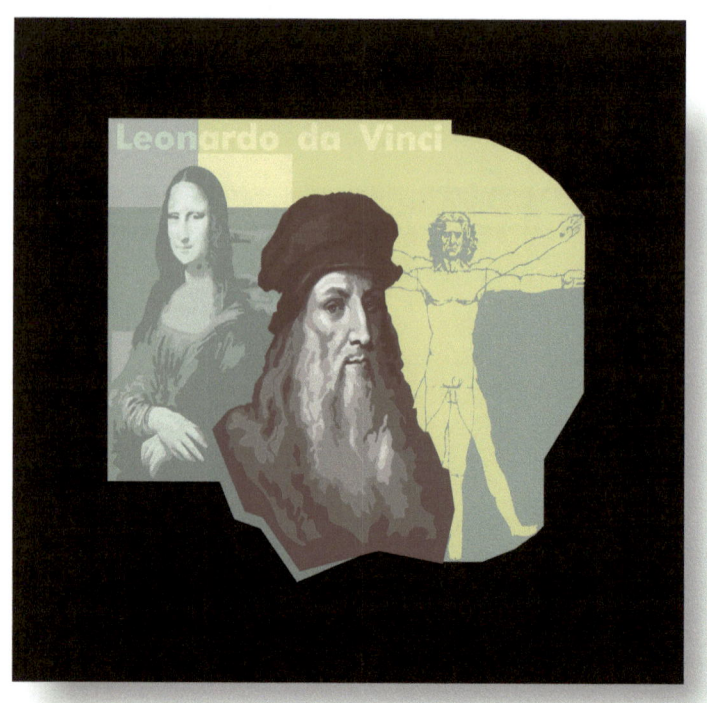

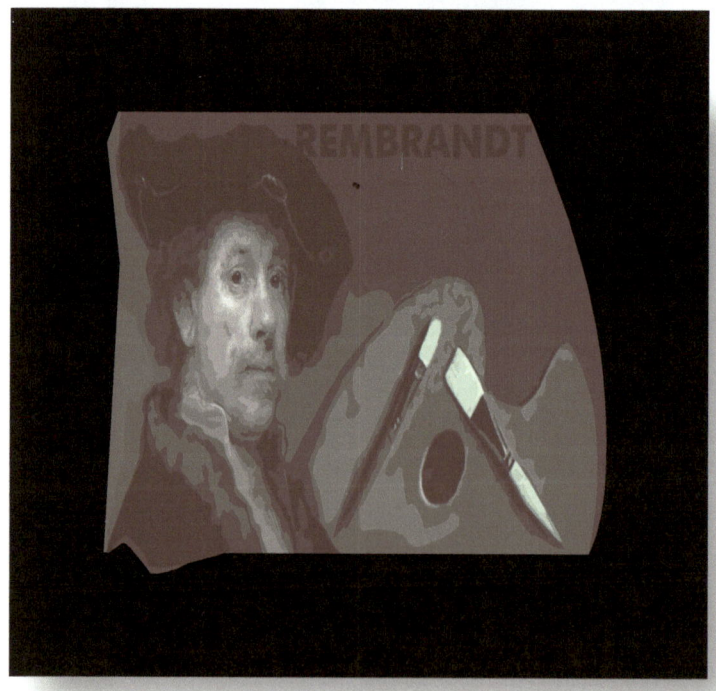

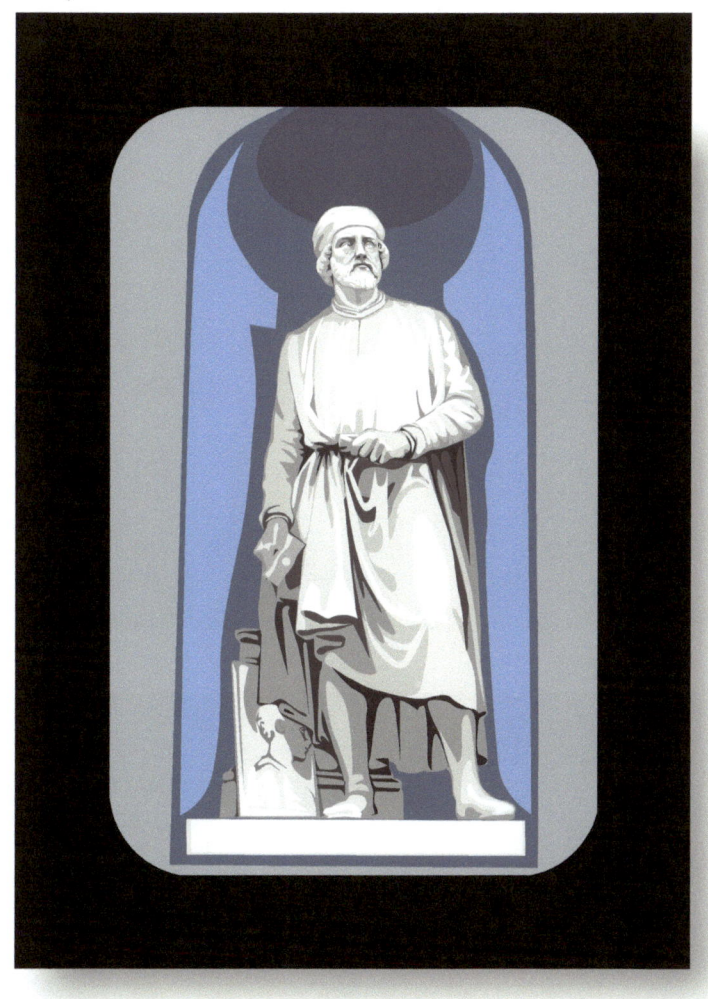

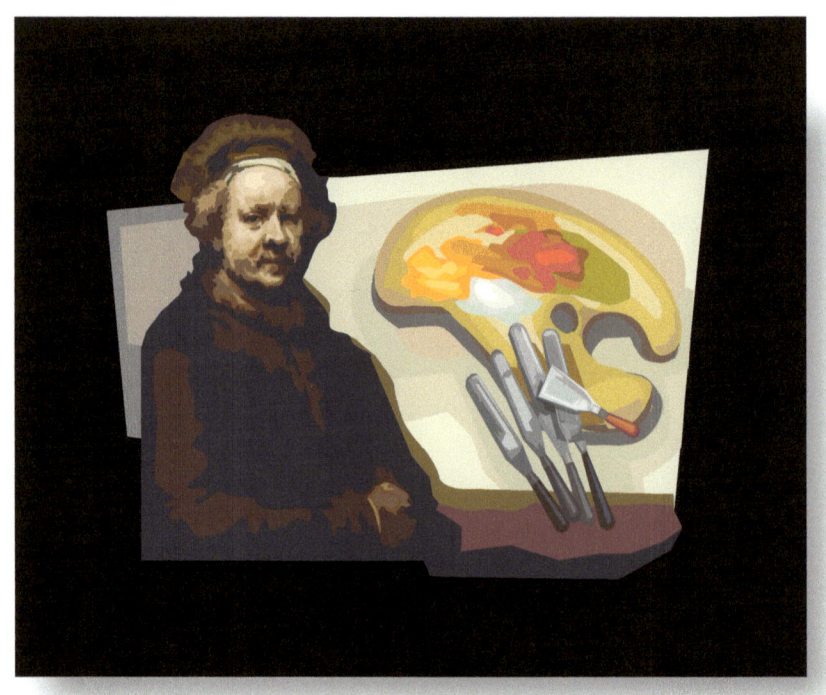

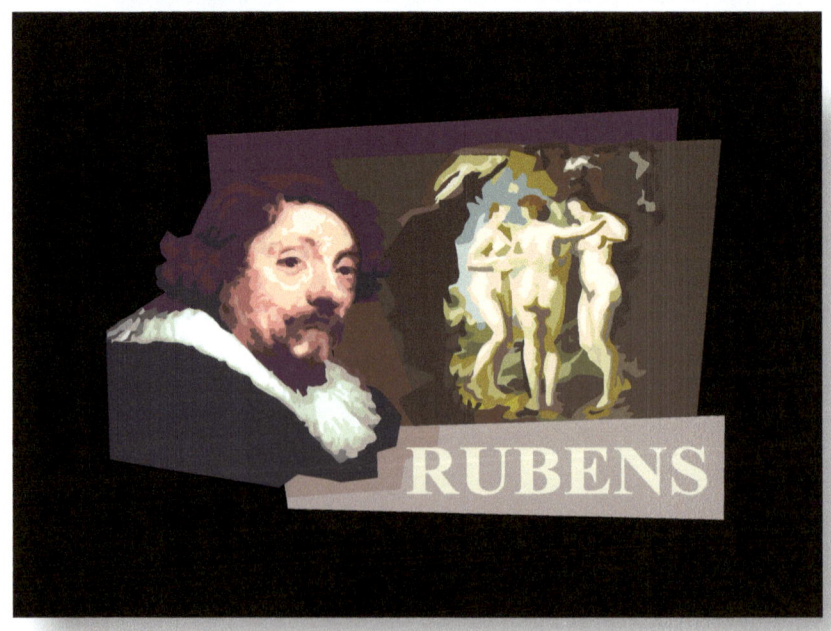

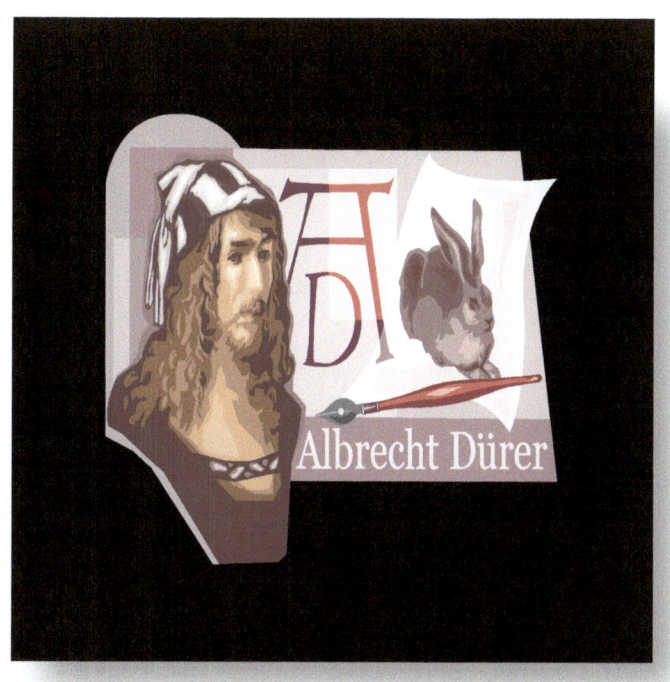

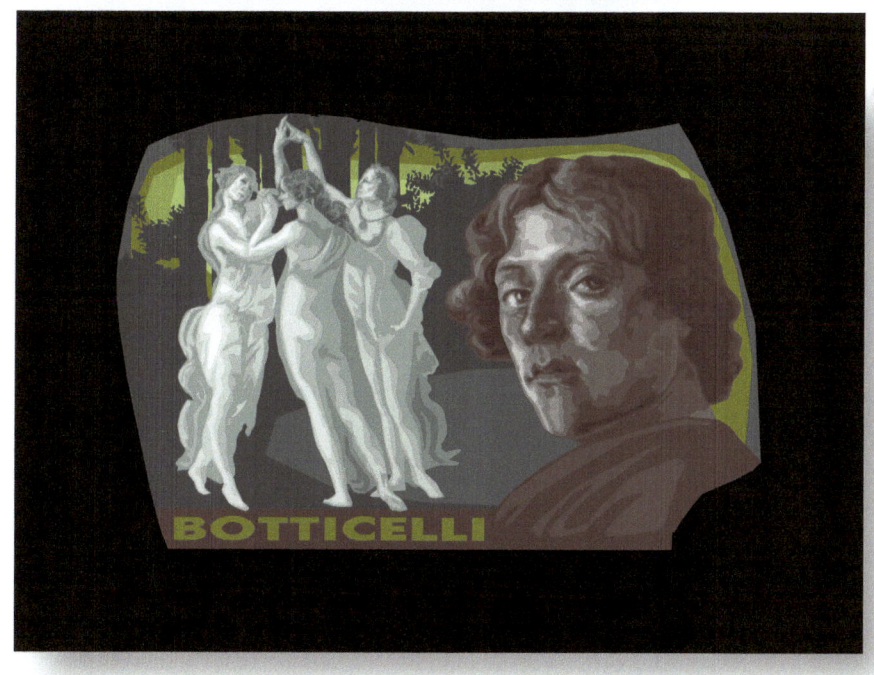

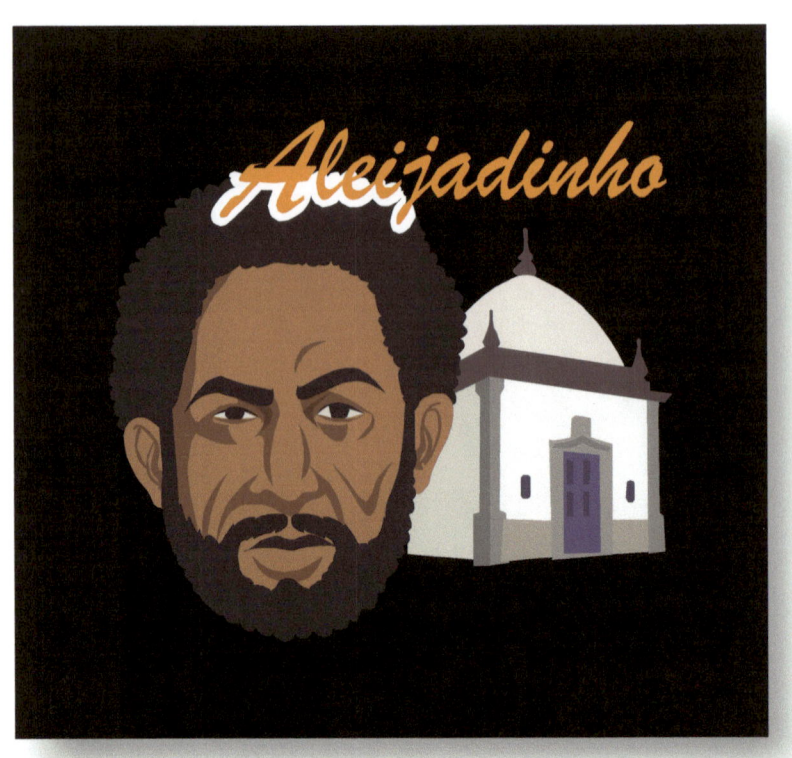

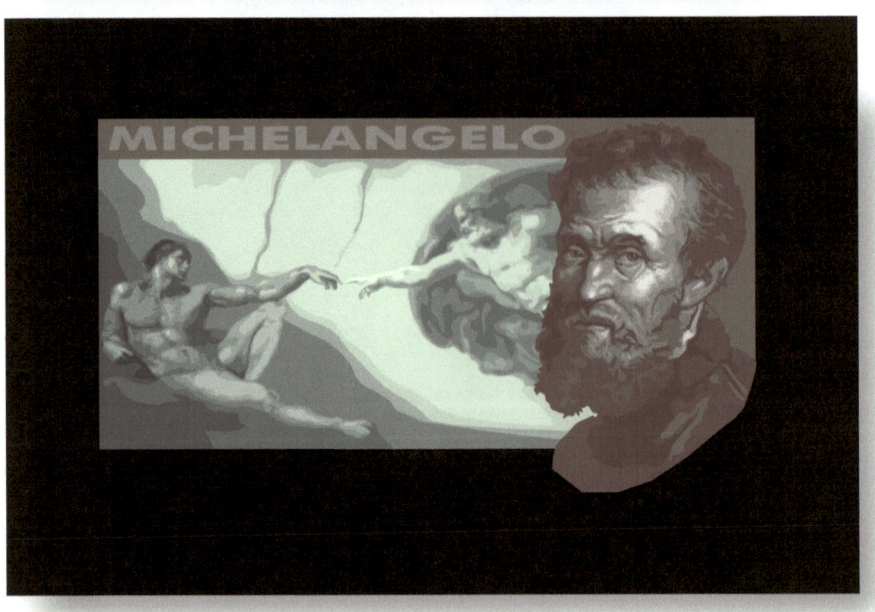

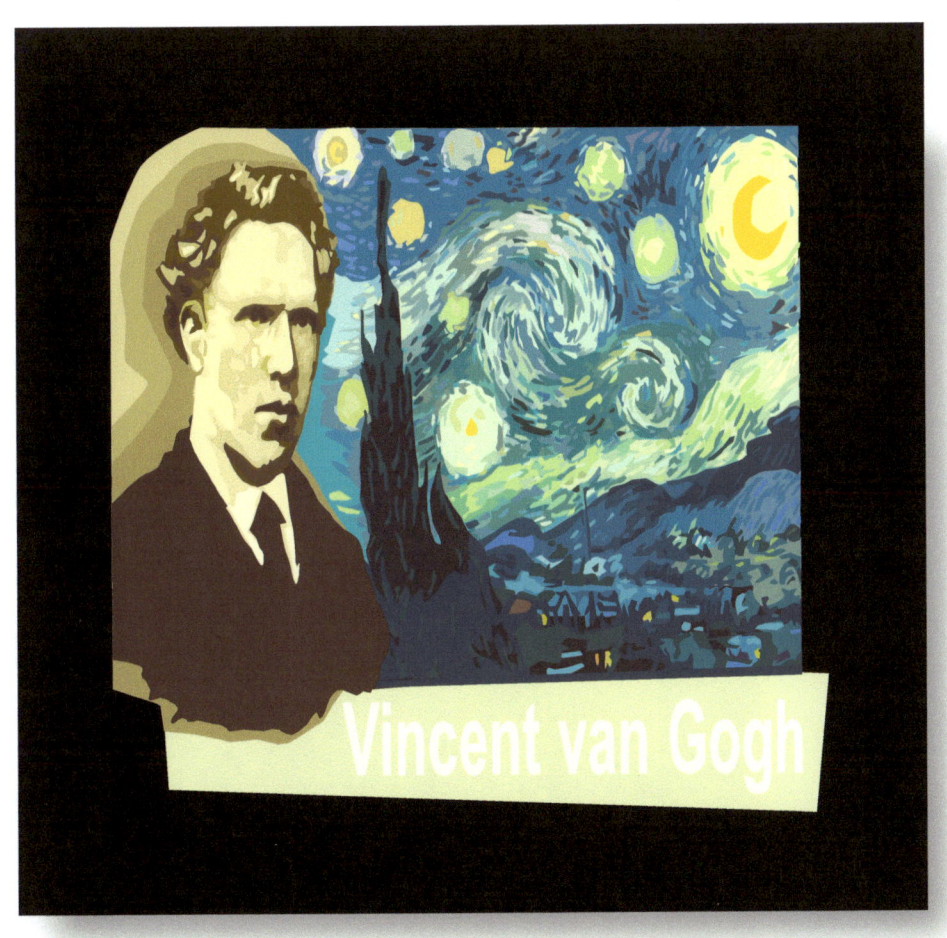

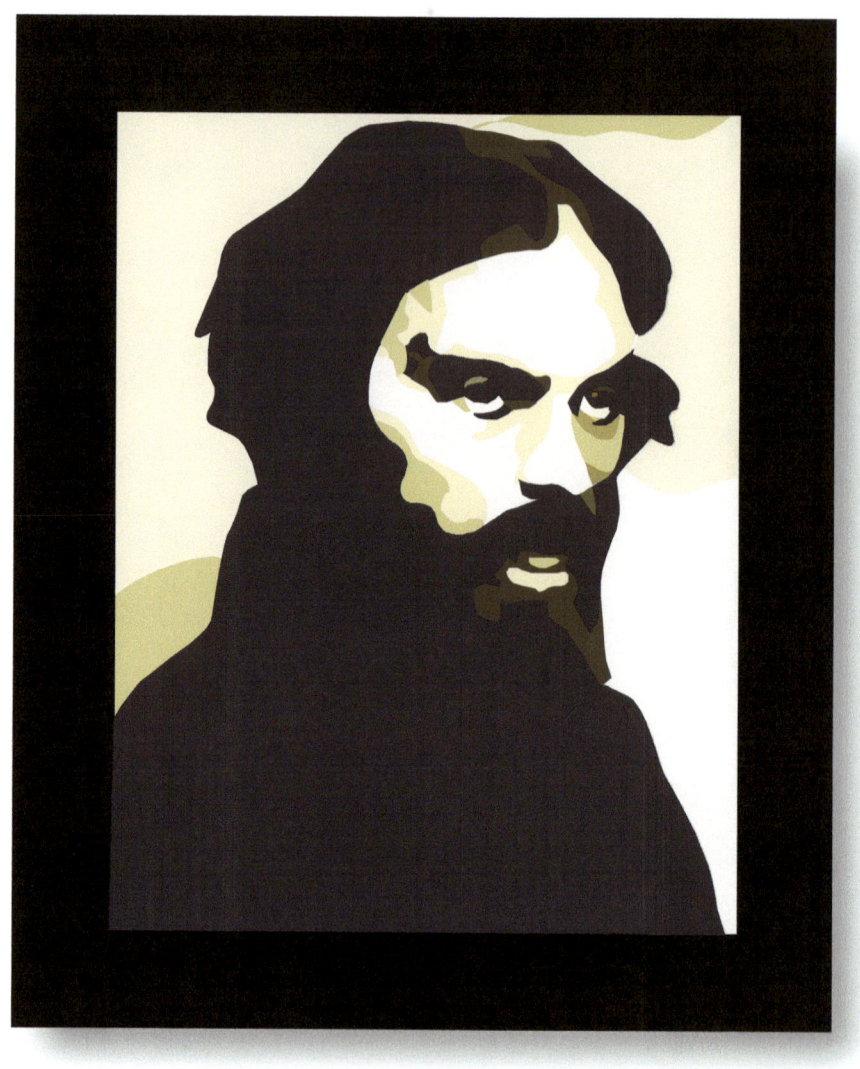

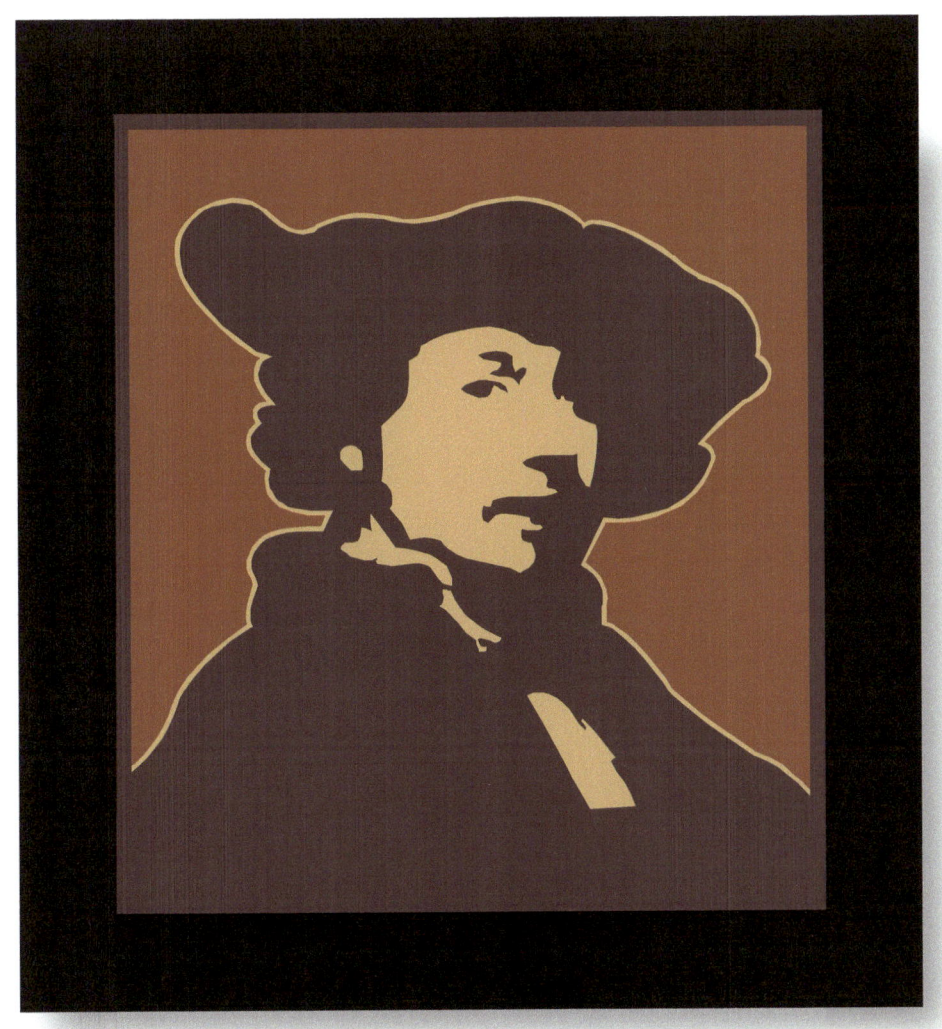

Artist, Dutch

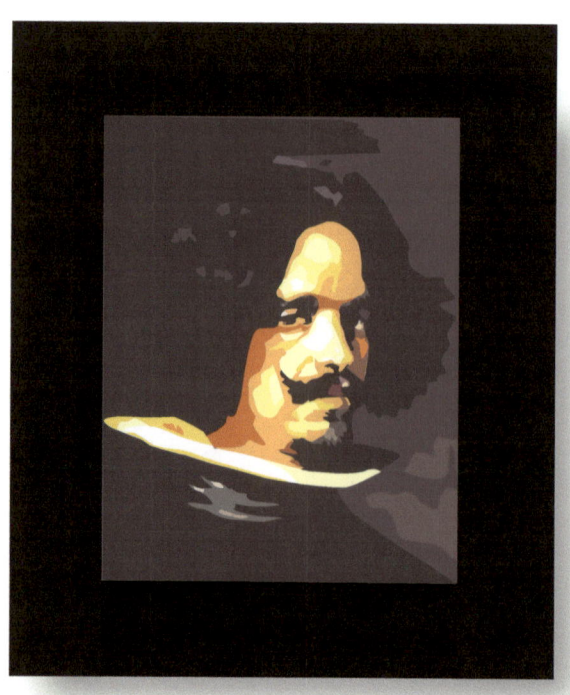

Artist,
Diego Velazquez, Europe

Artist, Bellini, Europe

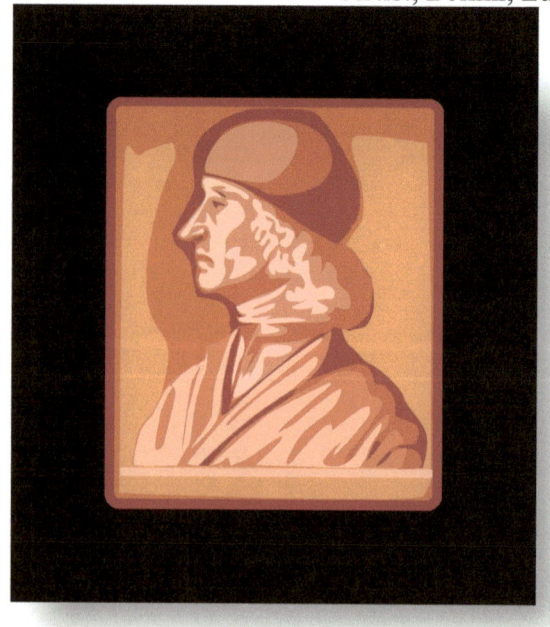

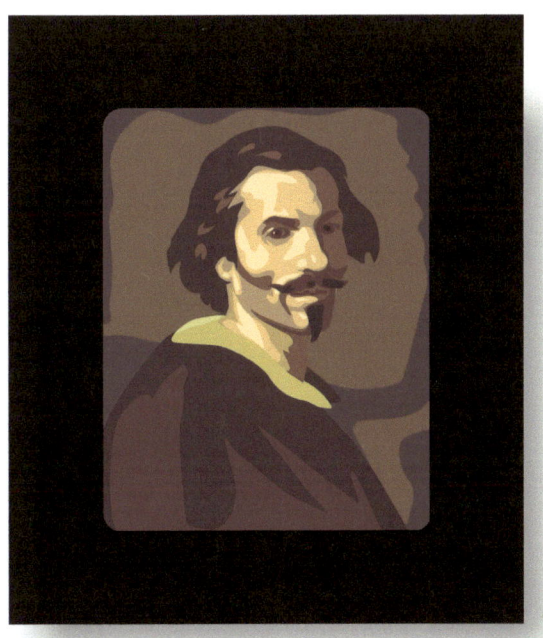

Artist, Baroque Bernini

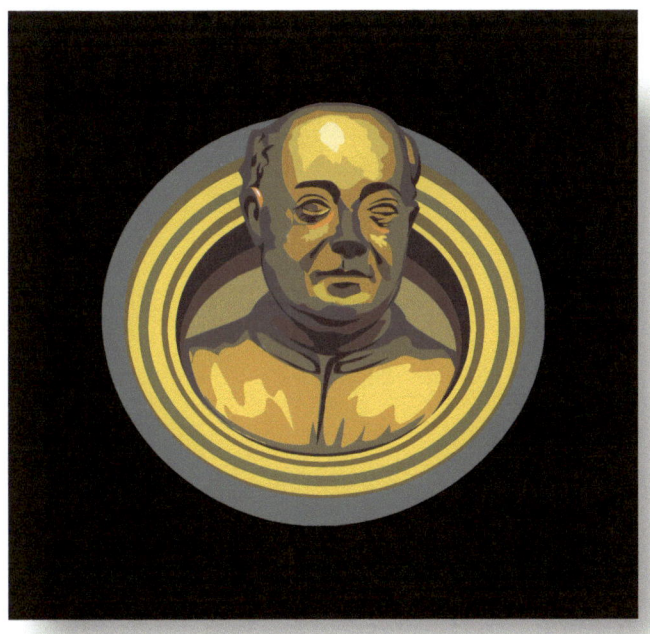

Artist, Europe

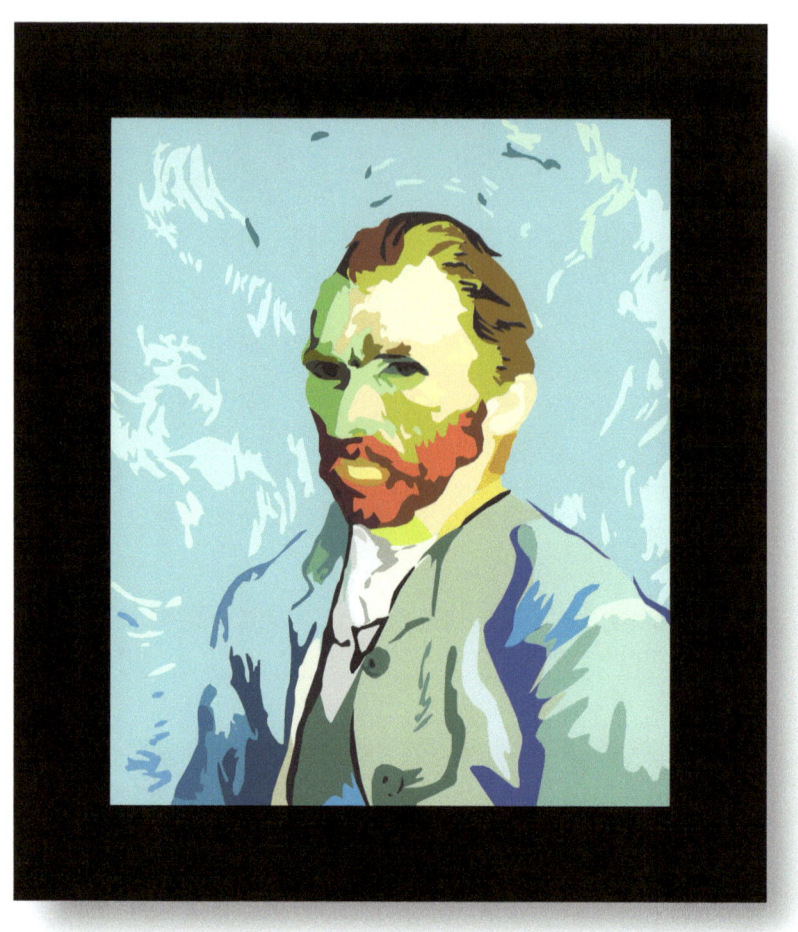

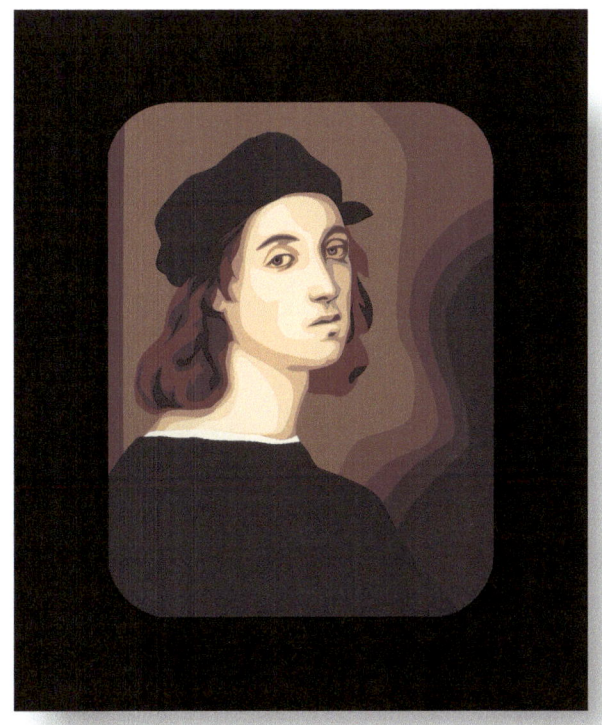

Artist, Europe

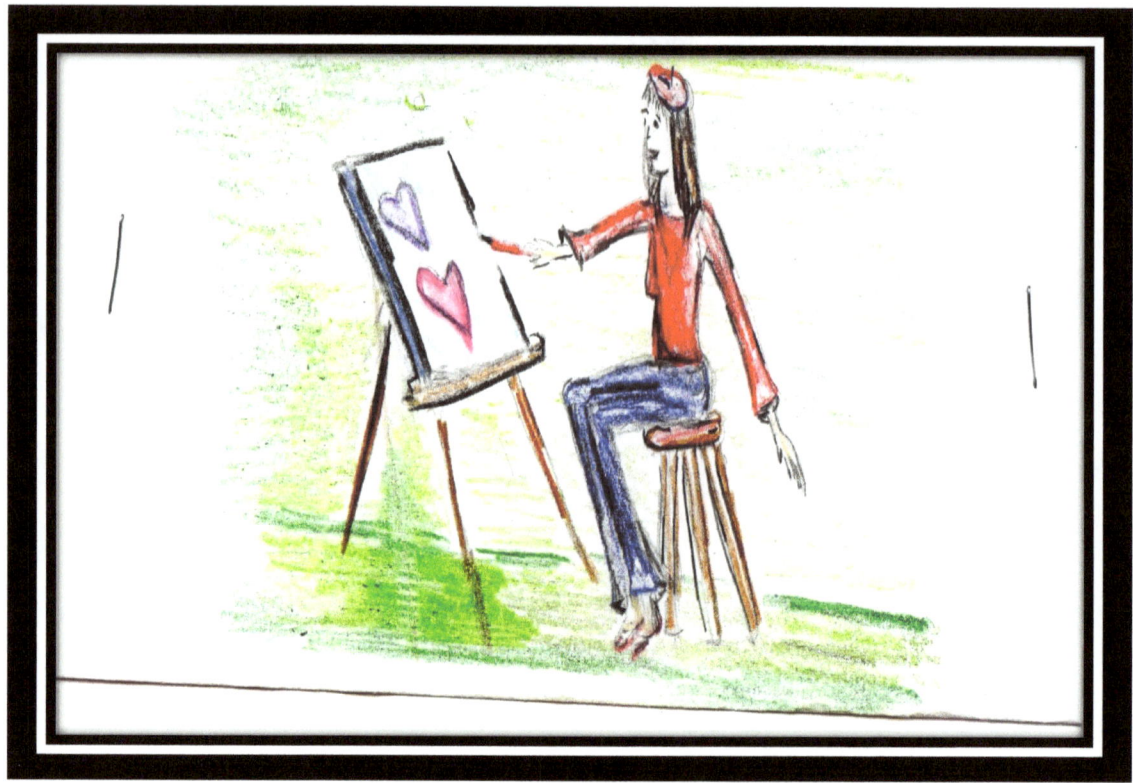

Charlotte would say to her Grandma "but I want to paint on my own one day". Paint perfectly. Charlotte has a feeling it might take her some hard work. Even though she has a talent to paint, her friends would tell her that she cannot just become an artist, she would have to go to a special School of Art. But she knows she has a natural talent for art with practice. She knows that she would be the best like her Grandma Bella one day.

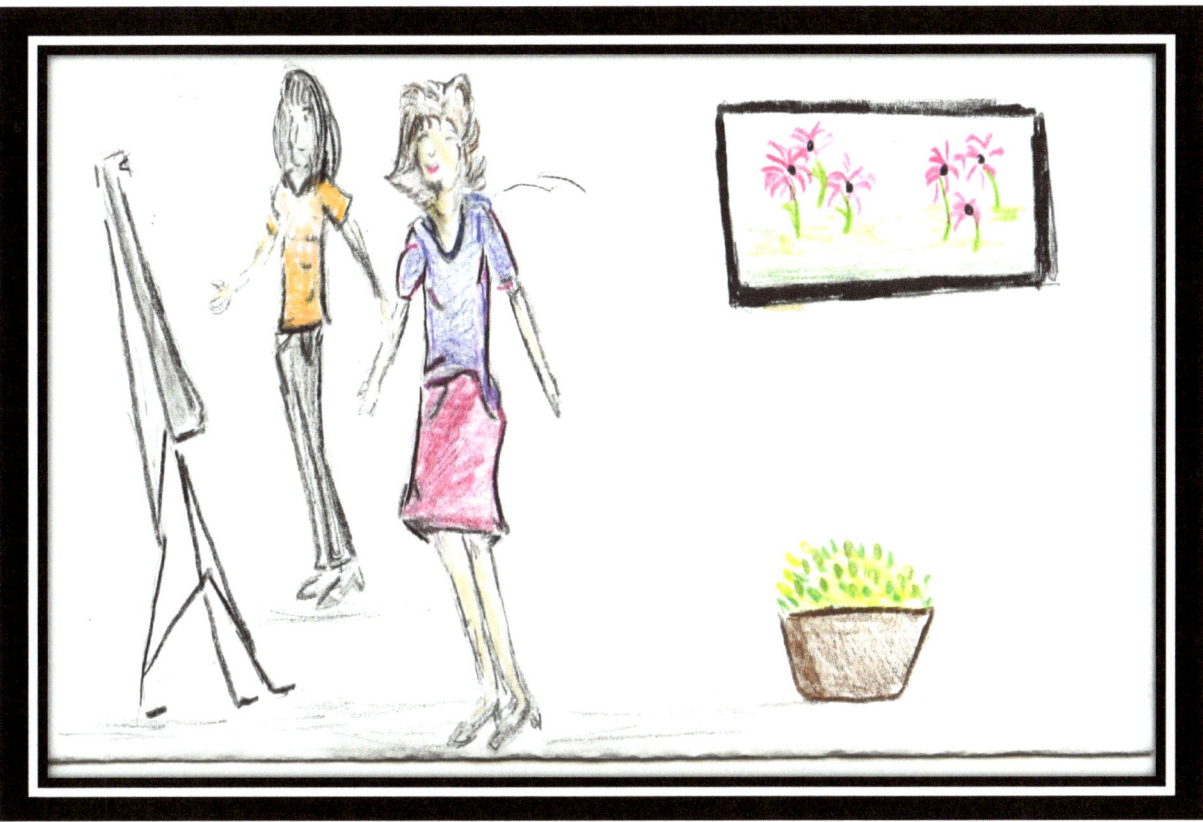

"Come on, Charlotte," her Grandma would say, "I have seen you paint when you were alone. You seem to love it, plus you are a very good artist. Won't you come paint with me in my studio?" Sometimes Charlotte finds the courage to join her Grandma in her painting studio to paint with her Grandma. But then she would paint a bit and then start to feel frustrated comparing herself to her Grandma. Her paintings do not seem as good as her Grandma's.

Her Grandma would always encourage her to keep going with her painting but Charlotte simply gave up.

One day, Charlotte's Grandma receives a note from Charlotte's Art teacher, Mrs. Petrie. She is asked to come to the school. Charlotte comes with her Grandma to her art classroom. Her art teacher talks with her Grandma about her artwork.

She wants to say that she is trying but that she just does not think her paintings are good enough. Mrs. Petrie is very impressed with Charlotte's work and tells Grandma she wants Charlotte to enter the School Art Exhibit in April. Charlotte does not have enough confidence in her work, but Mrs. Petrie does. So they continue to talk about Charlotte's artwork and Charlotte goes outside to wait for her Grandma.

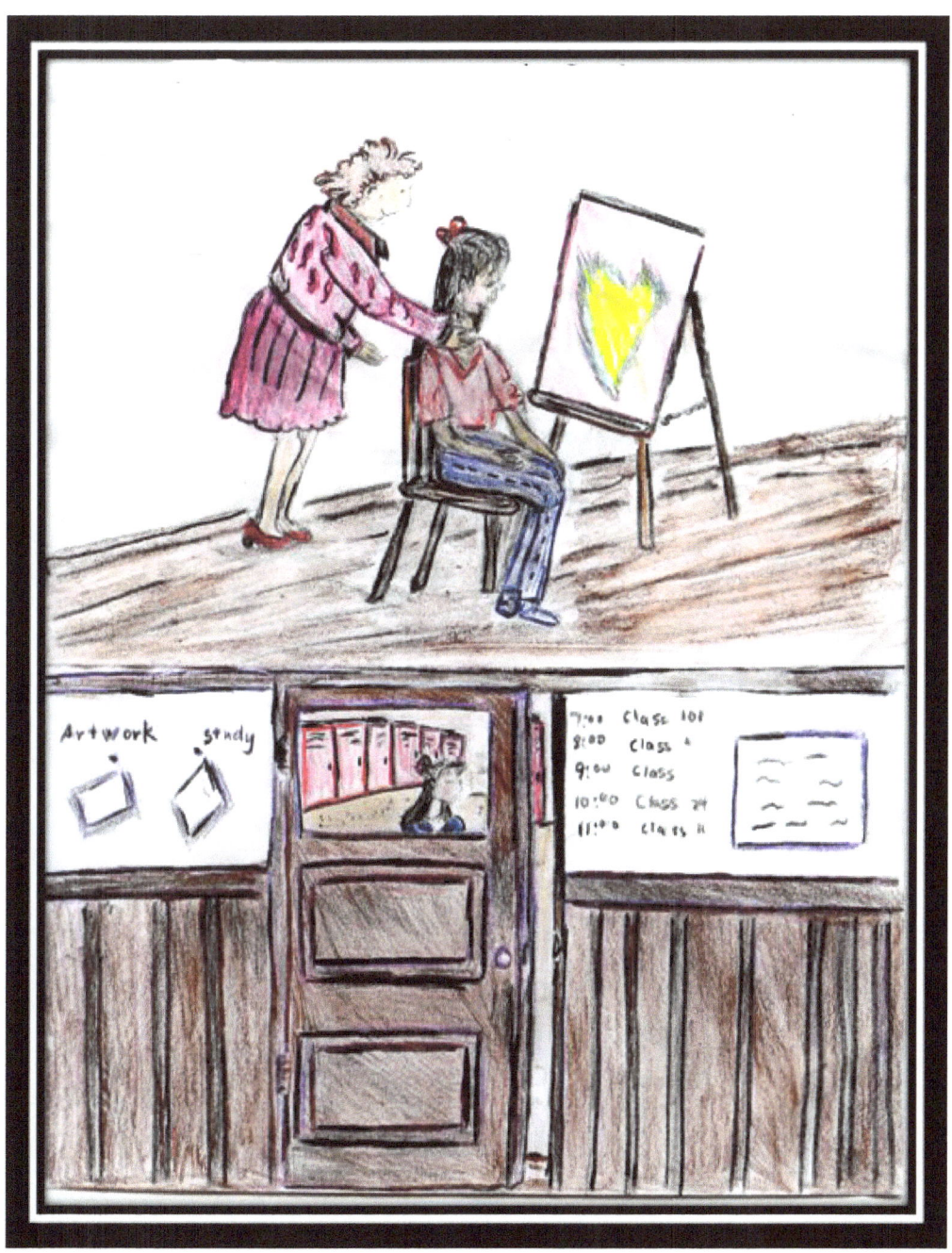

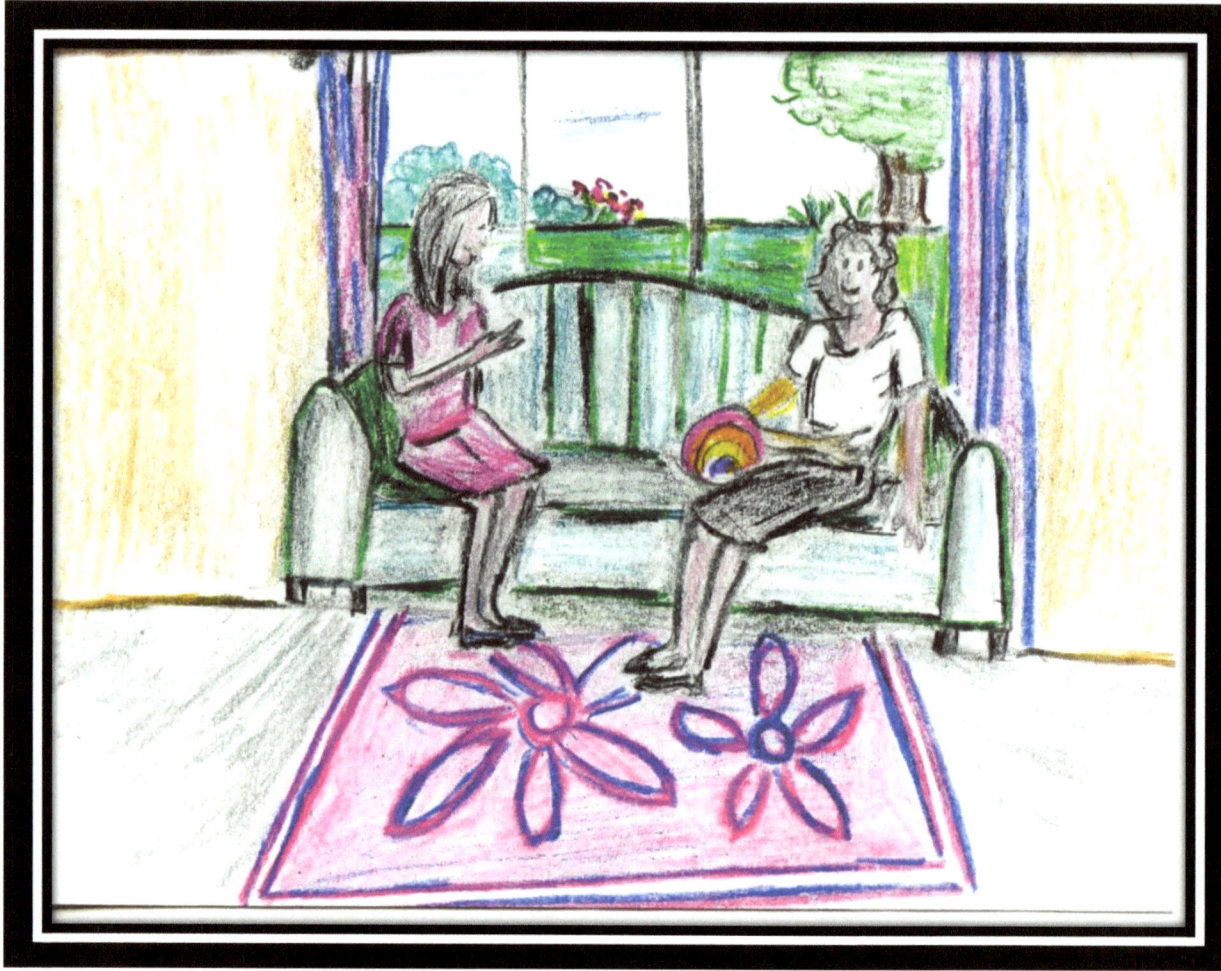

"Charlotte, I had a nice talk with Mrs. Petrie, your teacher". Grandma Bella begins to tell Charlotte about what her teacher talked with her about. "Mrs. Petrie thinks that you are an intelligent and very creative girl. She wants me to encourage you to enter into the Art Exhibit in the springtime. She thinks you can be a good artist with a little help".

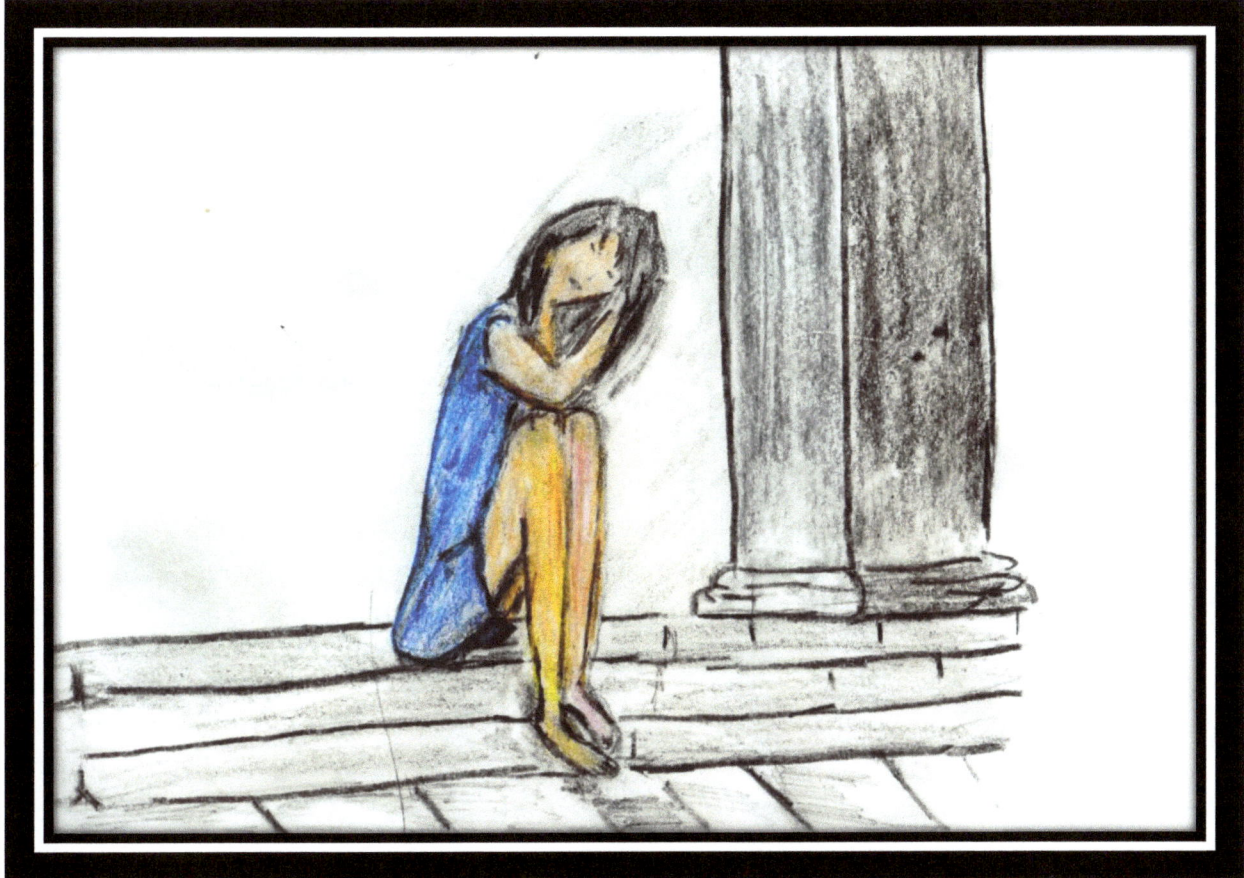

     Charlotte is feeling a bit ashamed that she was feeling the way she did about her art, knowing that it is a natural talent to have. "I will try harder" Charlotte says "but when I paint it just does not seem good enough. I make too many mistakes I think. That's why I do not like to show my artwork to others." "I will help you," says Charlotte's Grandma. "I know how you feel, because I used to feel that way a long time ago. I do not want you to feel that way. I want you to feel good about your paintings."

Charlotte says, "You paint all the time." "I've seen your paintings, you seem to love painting." "That's right," says Charlotte's Grandma. "It just took a little while to learn the proper strokes on how to paint on a canvas. I was just like you." She says with a smile and a pat on Charlotte's back. "Once you understand the proper strokes and brushes and other techniques, you will enhance your talent."

Charlotte and her Grandma would sit in her studio after homework and paint together. Grandma Bella would introduce her to various ways of different brush stroke techniques.

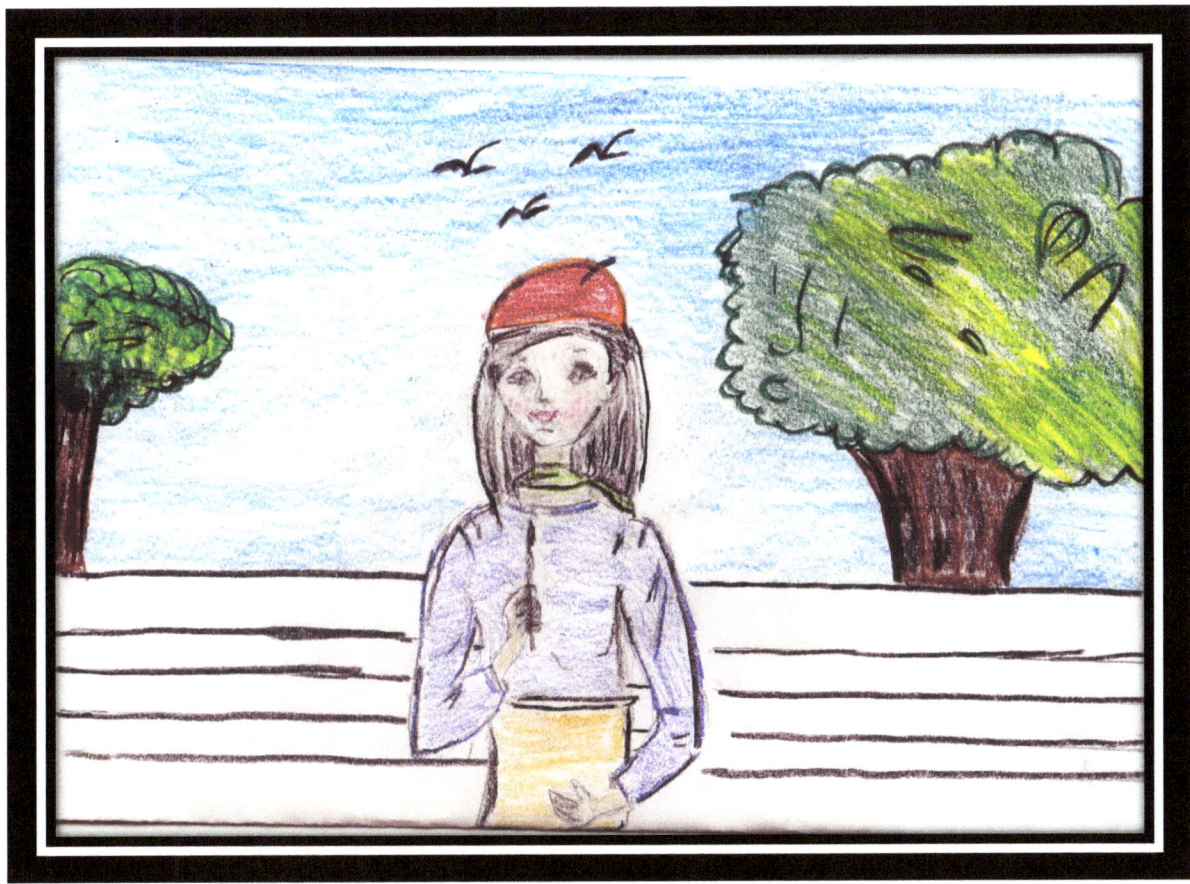

Charlotte begins to practice her painting techniques every evening. Sometimes during the evening after school her Grandma would take her out on the town to visit the town's Art Galleries as a treat. Grandma Bella is so proud of Charlotte and her desire to do better. She sees discipline in Charlotte and perseverance.

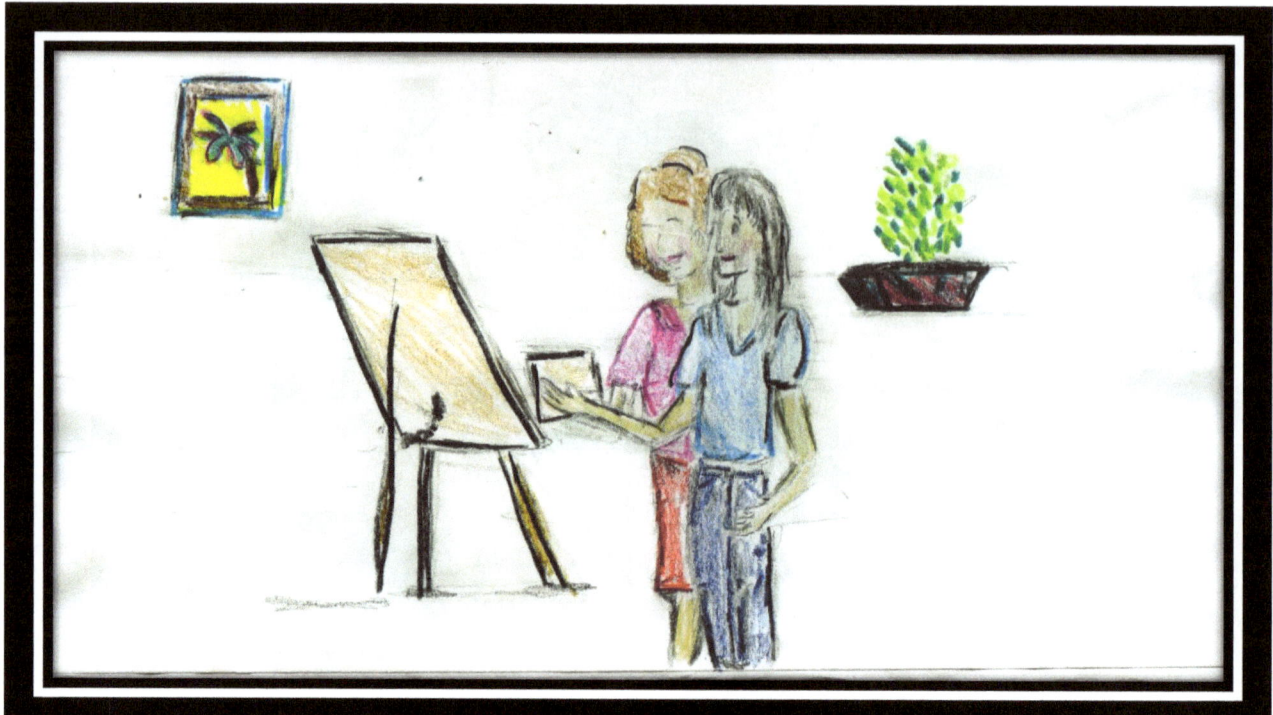

Her Grandma Bella compliments her on how nice her paintings look. Grandma says to Charlotte how cleverly she used some of the paints to create a calm affect in the sky in one of her paintings. She says, "You are learning so much and working so hard you will do well in the Art Exhibit in the spring." Charlotte continues to practice and learn from her Grandma.

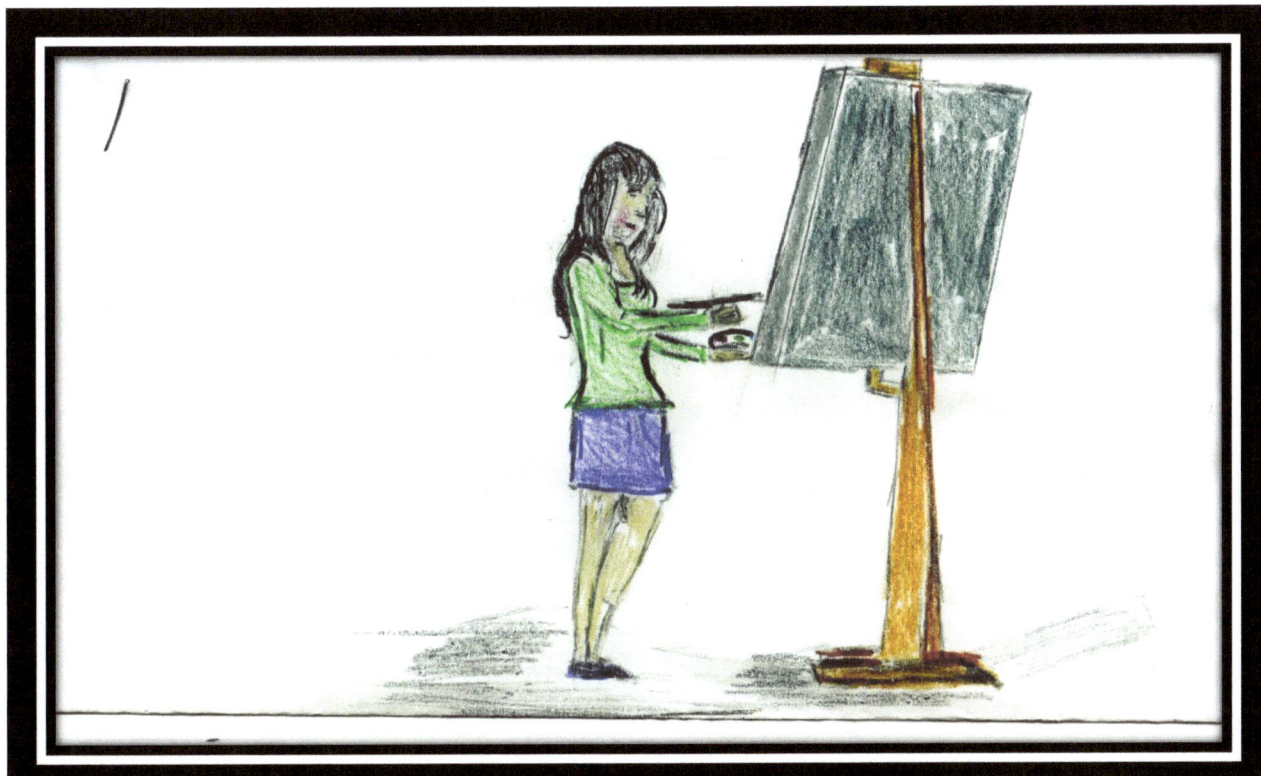

Sometimes her paintings would come out all wrong but she does not care, she would not give up. She knows that her paintings are getting better each time she paints. She becomes more confident in her ability to paint since practicing with her Grandma. She has a passing thought that everyone in her whole school would see her paintings. But since the art show was not for a few more weeks, Charlotte still has some time to practice her strokes.

Charlotte wants to learn as much as she can from her Grandma. Although Charlotte still is somewhat of a perfectionist, at times she wants it to be perfect but does not come down on herself so hard anymore. Her Grandma praises her when she does well and that gives her more confidence in herself.

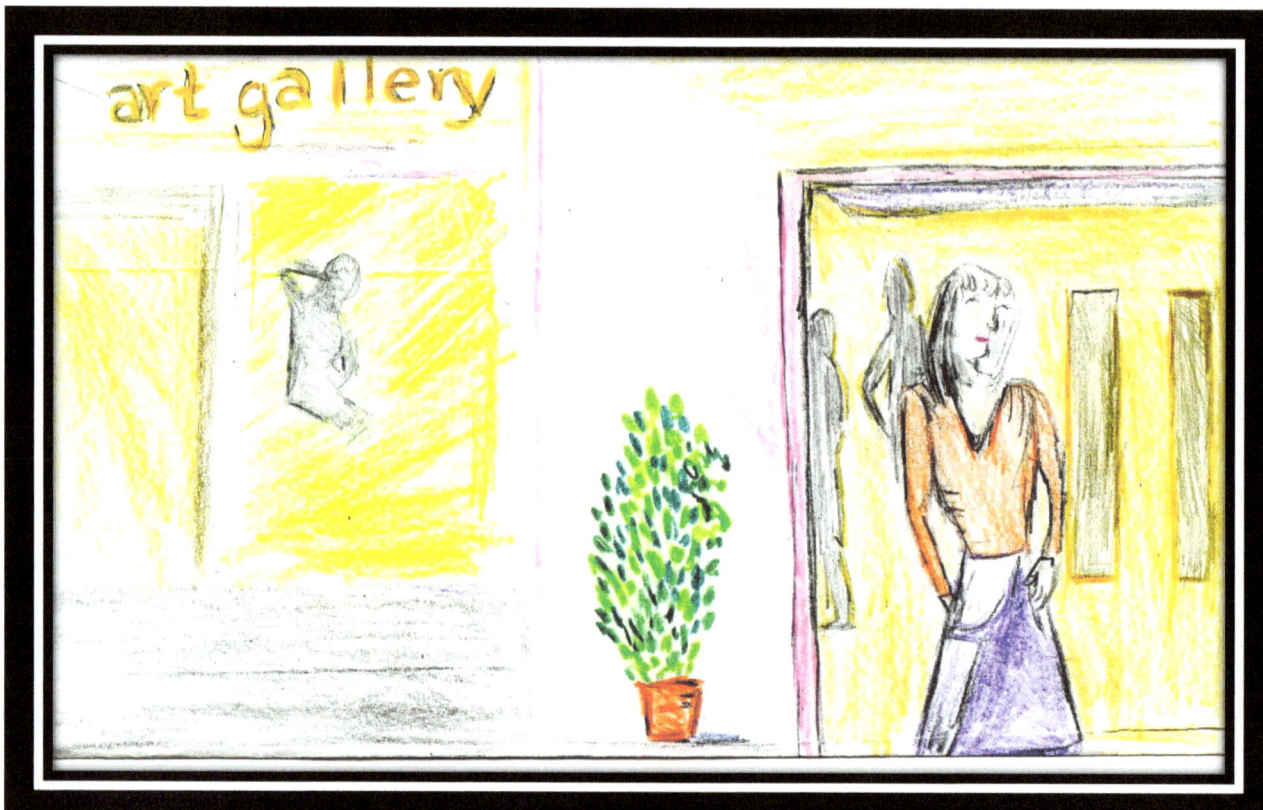

She takes her time for the spring show. Many weeks pass and then one day Charlotte's Grandma says "Charlotte, it is time to paint your painting that you want to enter into the contest in the Spring Art Exhibit".

The day of the spring show comes, and Charlotte's Grandma says "Good Luck! Your painting looks great!" Then Grandma goes to look at others with Charlotte's mom and dad along with Charlotte's best friends. They are all rallying for her to win.

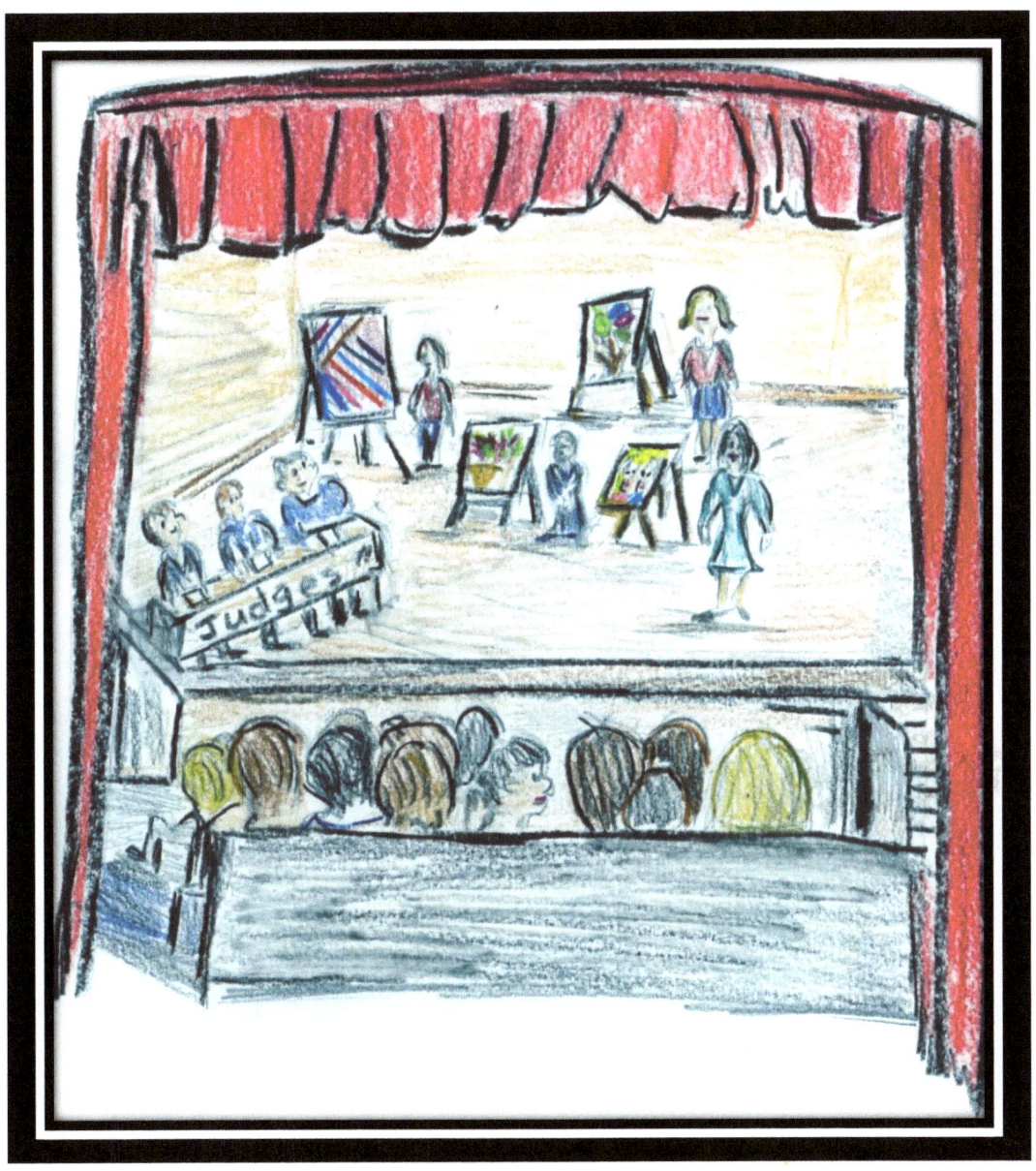

One by one the judges come to each contestant to judge their paintings. Then it is Charlotte's turn.

There are three judges, Mr. Glen, the Art Director from the Art Museum Grandma and her visited, the Mayor of Jeffersonville and of course, the principal, Mr. Moore.

They view each painting thoroughly, clinging to their tablets, so that no one could see the final results but them until it was revealed who was the winner. They go back to the judges' booth and compare their notes and begin to walk back to the stage. Very nervously, everybody stands by their Artwork.

Charlotte sees her Grandma looking at her with an encouraging smile. Charlotte gives her a nervous smile back.

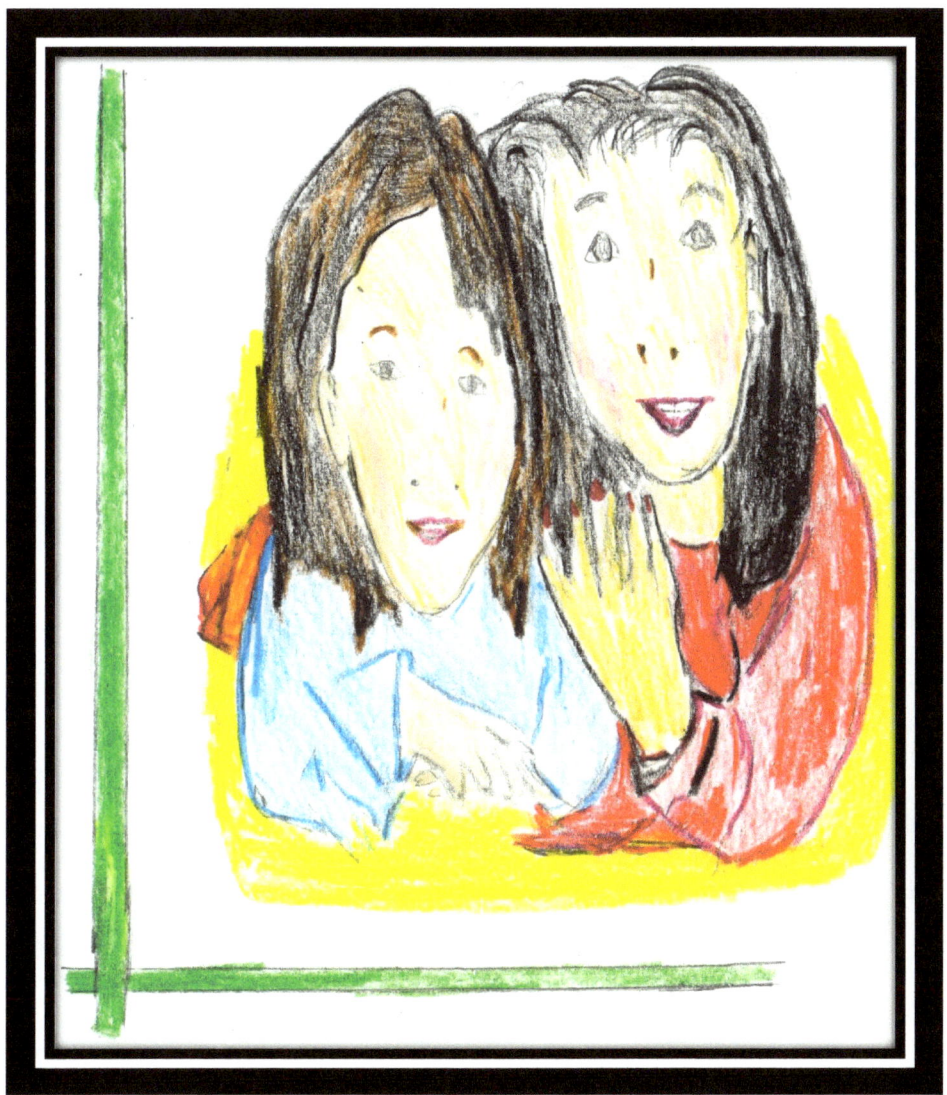

Charlotte calls her painting, "A Grandma's Love".

Charlotte's painting is so nice on her canvas. The judges come to her, carrying a blue ribbon placing it near her painting. Charlotte wins. She looks at her Grandma Bella and her mom and dad saying "I won! I won!" She is so excited, her Grandma comes over to congratulate her and she hugs her and says, "I knew you could do it."

Charlotte is so happy, she says, "I really won"!

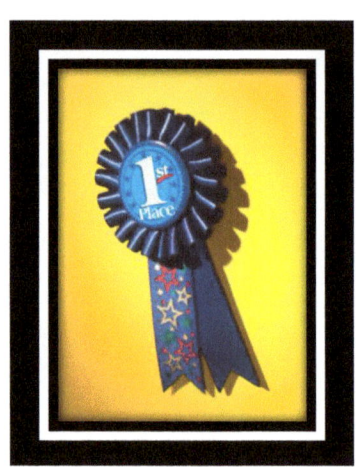

www.ingramcontent.com/pod-product-compliance
Lightning Source LLC
Chambersburg PA
CBHW050407180526
45159CB00005B/2177